DAY TRADING

A Quick and Easy Guide for Beginners to Start Day Trading

Pete Manlow

Table of Contents

Introduction

Thank you for taking the time to download this book "Day Trading: A quick and easy guide for beginners to start day trading".

This book is written to help individuals who are interested in embarking on a career in the rewarding yet risky field of day trading in the stock market.

Basically, the stock market, also known as the equity market, refers to the marketplace where traders can buy and sell stocks of companies that are publicly held. The trade can be done over-the-counter or through brokered exchanges.

The stock market is among the pillars of an economy based on free market principle, because it serves as the financial resource of companies who need capital and for investors who are interested in a stake of ownership in companies.

Through the stock market, anyone can grow small investments into sizeable ones, and to accumulate wealth without the need to start a business or devote most of your time and energy to your career.

Day trading refers to the buying and selling of stocks or shares in one trading day. This can be done in any marketplace, but it is common in the stock market as well as in the foreign exchange (forex) market.

Before you can become a successful day trader, you should master the basic strategies of stock trading, use advanced strategies to make profits every day, and have enough fund to trade large volumes of stocks.

As a day trader, you should be adept in using stock trading strategies and have a substantial amount of money at your disposal to make money on the small fluctuations in currencies or in highly liquid shares in the stock market.

Once again, thanks for downloading this book, I hope you find it to be helpful!

Chapter 1 - Introduction to the Stock Market

With the stock market, you can make or lose money according to the financial performance of the companies you invest in. If you buy stocks of a company and it becomes profitable, you can make money through dividends or by selling your stocks at a higher price, which is known as capital gain.

However, you can also lose money if you buy stocks of a company that fails to hit its financial targets. The price of the stocks will go down, so you will lose money if you decide to sell.

There are two primary sections of the stock market: the primary market and the secondary market.

New stocks are issued and sold through Initial Public Offering or IPO in the primary market. Large investors usually buy most IPO stocks from investment banks. The succeeding trades take place on the secondary market, where traders include both individual and institutional traders.

Company shares are traded through exchanges. In the United States, there are two main stock exchanges: The New York Stock Exchange (NYSE) established in 1792 and the NASDAQ, which was established in 1971 by the National Association of Securities Dealers (NASD) as the first electronic stock exchange.

Nowadays, most stock exchange trades are performed electronically through computers, and in fact, the stocks today are now held in digital form, and rarely as physical bonds.

In order to know the current performance of the stock market, you can refer to the index of stocks for the market segment or for the entire market such as Nasdaq index, Morgan Stanley Europe, Dow Jones Industrial Average, Standard and Poor's 500, Russell 2000, Far East Index and Australasia Index.

Should You Trade In the Stock Market?

It is common for beginners to doubt the idea of making money by trading in the stock market. Exaggerated claims for returns and popular stories of traders making a lot of money only to lose all of them in the market can really generate negative perception about stock trading.

This is why it is crucial to understand a bit more about the stock market and how it works before you decide to go into day trading.

First, let's learn about stocks and shares.

When you buy a stock, you are actually purchasing a share of the company. If a publicly held company wants to raise money, it will issue shares. This will be conducted through the IPO, in which the stock price is based on the estimated value of the company, and how many shares will be released. The company will receive the money raised to expand its operations, while the stocks will be traded on the stock exchange such as NASDAQ and NYSE.

Investors and traders continue to exchange company stocks, even though the company is no longer receiving capital from the trade. The company will only raise capital during the IPO.

Stock investors and traders continue to exchange stocks after the IPO because the estimated value of companies vary. Investors can gain or lose money depending on the perceived value in the market, which influences the movement in the price.

It is often difficult to project which specific stock will increase or decrease in value at a specific period. In general, stocks have the tendency to rise, which is the reason why most investors are choosing to purchase stocks in different sectors, or diversify the investment, and keep them for a long period.

Many investors who are trading in this method are not concerned about the small movements in the stock prices. Their ultimate objective of purchasing shares is to make money by purchasing stocks in companies that are expected to perform remarkably or those whose estimated value in the market are expected to grow.

You can also earn money through dividends released by companies that are already established, usually companies who have been in the industry for decades and even centuries. The dividend refers to the percentage of the company's revenue, which the company releases to its shareholders.

The price of the stocks also tends to fluctuate, and the gains and losses linked with the stock price are not dependent on the dividend. There can be minimal or substantial dividends, and they may not even exist as listed companies are not required to pay dividends. Investors who are looking for regular profit from stock market trading usually prefer purchasing stocks that are also paying dividends.

If you buy company shares, you are owning a percentage of the company and so you might have a say on how it operates. Although there are varieties of shares (a company may choose to release shares several times), usually owning shares can provide you voting rights that are equal to the number of shares that you own. In general, shareholders are allowed to choose the board of directors and may even be allowed to vote on crucial decisions that the company has to make.

Why Trade Stocks

In every stock trade, there should be a seller and a buyer. If you purchase 100 stocks (known as a lot), someone is actually selling 100 shares to you. The seller or the buyer could be passive or aggressive, which influences the price.

If the stock prices are falling, sellers are usually aggressive to trade because they want to sell their shares at a cheaper price. Meanwhile, the buyers are described as passive and could only be willing to purchase at cheaper prices. The price shall continue to fall until the price will reach a point that buyers are becoming more aggressive to purchase at higher prices, which will influence the price further.

Not all traders behave like this, which could lead some investors selling shares at various times. A trader may keep stocks that has matured remarkably in price and may choose to sell to lock in the revenue and receive the cash. Another investor might have purchased at a higher price compared to current price, which places the investor in a loose end. That investor could sell to maintain the loss from getting bigger. Traders and investors could also sell as they may project that the stock will further go down based on their research strategies and so they may want to sell the shares before the price falls down further.

Stock Volume

In the stock market, volume refers to how many shares are exchanged in a trading day. Most stocks on main exchanges like NASDAQ and NYSE are exchanging millions of stocks every day. This means that possibly, hundreds of thousands of traders are deciding to buy or sell their shares on any given day. Stocks that are receiving high volume are enticing for investors, because the volume could mean that they can trade their shares anytime.

It is still possible to sell a small number of stocks even if no one is actively exchanging their shares or if the volume is not enough as the stock market is required to provide volume. These investors are usually known as market makers, and they buy and sell stocks if there is not enough traders for the day. However, they must not influence the prices of stocks, which is why many traders still prefer to trade stocks with great volumes, and so they don't depend on these market makers. Today, most market makers are already digital and automated. But still, you can find actual people on NYSE, usually wearing blue jackets, but they are working to trade shares for specific firms and also help in processing public stock orders.

Conclusion

Companies can raise capital by issuing stocks, and the stock will then continue to be exchanged on the market. In general, stocks tend to rise in long-term, which makes it rewarding to own shares. You can also gain added benefits from dividends, voting rights, and potential gains. The prices of stock may fall, so most traders prefer to invest in diversified shares, which will lessen the risk of losing all their investments in one go. Stocks can be traded or purchased at any given time, as long as there is sufficient volume to process the transaction.

Now that we have introduced you to the world of stock market, it is time to learn about day trading, which we will discuss in the next chapter.

Chapter 2 - Introduction to Day Trading

Day trading refers to the act of buying or selling stocks or shares in one trading day. This can be done in any marketplace, but it is often in the stock market as well as foreign exchange (forex) market.

Before you can become a successful day trader, you should master the basic strategies of stock trading, use advanced strategies to make profits every day, and have enough fund to trade large volumes of stocks.

Day traders are masters in using stock trading strategies and have substantial amount of money at their disposal to make money on the small fluctuations in currencies or in highly liquid shares in the stock market.

There are two primary functions of day traders in the marketplace:

1. They drive the liquidity of the marketplaces, particularly in the stock market; and

2. They sustain the operations of the markets through arbitrage

This chapter will take an objective perspective at day trading, the traders who are practicing it, and how you can try it to make profit.

Day Trading Misconceptions

There is some sort of controversy when it comes to day trading. The revenue potential of day trading is actually among the most controversial subjects on stock exchanges. This is mainly because of the fact that numerous online scams have pushed these misconceptions by claiming that anyone can make huge amounts of money in a day through day trading.

On the other hand, some financial "gurus" continue to promote this kind of trading as an easy way to make money, which works all the time. The veracity of such claims is actually in the middle ground. There are traders who participate in day trading without enough background knowledge (they are more of gamblers than traders), while there are also traders who actually make a lot of money.

Some financial experts as well as fund managers are also not interested in day trading, because they believe that the possible returns are not justifiable if you consider the risk. They even claim that there are no popular day traders, while famous investors such as Peter Lynch and Warren Buffett are living proofs that it is more lucrative to trade through conventional approach.

Meanwhile, those who participate in day trading insist that you can make substantial profits if you know what to do. They claim that the success ratio is naturally lower because of the complicated system and the inherent risk in day trading.

In general, the stock market is not united on this concern, but it is a common agreement that day trading is not for all, and it could be risky. Furthermore, it requires great deal of understanding of the dynamics of the stock market as well as keen use of different strategies in making profits for the short term.

Who Is a Day Trader?

This book will concentrate on people who are into day trading every day of their lives. We call them professional day traders. Those who are only trading in the stock market once in a while are hobbyists. Day traders are usually veterans in the field, and have accumulated enough knowledge of the stock exchange. Below are some of the common characteristics of professional day traders:

Knowledgeable and Expert in the Stock Market

Traders who try to practice day trading without enough knowledge and expertise of fundamental stock trading could lose a lot of money.

With Enough Capital to Lose

Yes, that's correct. You cannot expect to make any profit through day trading. Those who are into day trading use money that they are willing to lose. This will not only safeguard you from financial disaster, but it can also help you to ditch away your emotions when you are engaged in day trading. A substantial amount of capital is usually needed to effectively capitalize on day to day fluctuations in the stock market.

Strategic

A day trader should have an advantage over other traders in the market. You will later learn about the common effective strategies in day trading. These strategies have been well in place and they usually result to consistent revenue and avoid substantial losses.

<u>Disciplined</u>

A strategy deemed effective will still be useless without discipline. Most day traders eventually lose substantial money as they have failed to secure exchanges that are clear in their requirements. Remember to stick to the plan and remember to follow your discipline.

Day Trading As a Profession

There are two main types of professional day traders: those who are trading in behalf of a stock investment company and those who are working alone. Most day traders are working for an investment company, and they have a lot of advantages such as easy access to a trading platform, substantial amount of capital as well as leverage, high-tech stock analysis software, and more. These traders are usually individuals who are looking for easy profits, which could be made through news events or opportunities for arbitrage. The resources to which these professional traders have access provide them the capacity to capitalize on trades that are less risky even before individual traders could respond.

Individual traders usually manage other people's funds or they just trade on their own. Very few of them can access a trading platform but they have connections with brokerage firms mainly because of high volumes of spending on commission and they also have access to other resources.

But the limited range of these resources hinder them from directly competing with institutional day traders, rather they are driven to manage with more risks. Individual day traders usually perform the trade through swing trades and technical analysis - integrated with some form of leverage - to generate enough revenue on minimal price fluctuations in stocks with high liquidity.

Essential Financial Services and Tools for Day Traders

Day trading can be profitable if you know how to use effective financial services and tools that are especially designed for stock market. As a day trader, you may need the following:

Software for Trading Analysis

A software capable of analyzing trends in the stock market is an expensive yet effective requirement for day traders. Traders who depend on swing trades or technical indicators depend more on software than industry news. Most software usually contain several features such as:

Automated Pattern Recognition

The capacity to identify technical indicators such as channels, flags, and even more complicated signifiers such as patterns known as Elliott Wave.

Broker Integration

These are programs that use neural networks and genetic algorithms to stabilize trading networks to increase accuracy in predictions for future price movements.

Back Testing

This feature will let you take a peek at how a specific strategy will perform in the past so you can project with more accuracy. But take note that previous performance doesn't always guarantee certain results.

Trading Desk Access

This is often used by institutional day traders who are trading in behalf of big trading companies or those who are trading huge funds. The trading desk makes it easy for traders to exchange stocks, which is crucial, specifically during sharp price fluctuations. For instance, when a company announces acquisition, day traders who are looking on the arbitrage for the merge could easily execute their orders hours before the rest of the stock market reacts.

News Sources

Credible information and news are important commodities in stock exchange. Day traders capitalize on news to project the price fluctuations, so it is essential to be the first to know if something is about to happen, is happening, or happened. The usual day trading office is always tuned into Dow Jones News and there are also several televisions that are tuned into CNBC, CNN, ABC, and other news agencies. Some day traders are also running software that analyzes streams of headlines and news for crucial stories.

Day traders who are keen in using these tools have more advantage over the rest of the traders. You may find it easy to make profits in day trading if you are familiar in using the tools described above.

Conclusion

Even though day trading has become sort of a controversial way to make money in the stock market, there is no way to deny that it is still a prevalent and profitable financial practice. Day traders, both individual and institutional, are actually crucial players in the market because they sustain the liquidity and efficiency of the exchange. Some believe that ordinary stock traders should stay away from day trading, while others claim that you can make substantial money if you know what to do and if you are armed with the right tools.

Chapter 3 - Getting Started in Day Trading

There are many obstacles that you have to overcome when you want to get started with day trading and begin making profits. Fortunately, most of these obstacles become a lot easier to handle when you are already familiar with the whole system and you are well prepared. Hence, this chapter will cover the common obstacles that you may encounter on the road.

Choosing the Right Day Trading Broker

It is crucial to consider your current day trading broker, if you are presently working with one. As it is recommended not to jump right away into day trading without enough knowledge of trading in its basic platforms. The first step that you need to take before you begin day trading is to make certain that your broker is suitable for your growing trading needs. If you decide to wait until you realize that you are losing money, the loss could be already substantial. So, it is ideal to find the right day trading broker as early as possible.

Consider Your Special Preferences in Day Trading

It is also crucial to figure out the features that your broker will provide when you are looking for a broker. Although most traders don't have any special preferences, if you have special requirements, you should consider that early on. Once you cover the basic of stock trading, the next step is to begin looking closer at different options.

Basically, you have to consider the fees and charges for each trade, as the general trade cost can be very high. Remember, the fees and charges may not only cover the trade commissions, but also other fees such as withdrawal fees, platform fees, and idle fees.

Moreover, there are brokers who are placing added restrictions that you should meet if you are interested in day trading, which includes validation of trading capacity or remarkably increased minimum balance. This restriction is often regarded as a way to avoid the image of taking advantage of day traders who are not fully informed.

Also, you have to figure out the leverage levels if you are interested to day trade in the stock market or the forex market or the margins for the futures market. You should also review the available promotions that the trading broker is presently offering and ensure that you read and understand the fine print.

Do Your Due Diligence

After narrowing down your search for possible brokers you want to work with, the next step is to look closer into the firms and ensure that they are competent and can deliver results. In the US, you have to check the broker's reputation with the Financial Industry Regulatory Authority for the stock market. If you are looking for futures or forex brokers, you have to consult the National Future Association. These industry bodies check the brokers and you can ask for data if a particular broker is currently facing unethical charges or violated broker standards. Beyond that, you should also check customer reviews and find out how they provide their services.

Trading brokers in the US are usually regulated by an industry body that regularly keeps them under scrutiny, especially for customer service. If you are interested to work with an overseas broker, you can land better deals and get access to trading platforms at a lower cost. But there is always a risk, because there may not be enough regulatory bodies outside the US to ensure that the broker is working ethically.

This is crucial for new traders as choosing regulated brokers will prevent fraud. Although we don't say that brokers who are unregulated are out there to rip you off. However, it is still better to be safe than to be sorry.

Call Your Broker

If you are an individual day trader, and you are just starting in the field, you will make most of your trades through the Internet. So, time will come that you will need to call your broker if you encounter some problems mostly about the trading platform you are using online. It is ideal to work this out with an actual customer service representative early on.

To make certain that the broker's customer service is existent and functional, you should call them and say that you are interested to learn more about their business. Try leaving a message. If there is no call back within 24 hours, then you should look elsewhere as it is a clear sign that they are not looking into the welfare of their clients. If you get into contact with a customer service representative, try calling them back again with any concern. This is to see how the brokerage will handle it and ensure that they are living up to their first impressions.

Gird Your Loins in Day Trading

After choosing a broker that you think is most suitable for your trading needs, the next step is to transfer funds to your trading account for the minimum balance. This is to make certain that if things are still not working out, you only have to deal with getting a reasonable cost back from the brokerage. Your trust with the broker firm will increase after several trades, so you can confidently increase the amount of your fund for trading.

But be sure to still be cautious when it comes to trading. You should still be wary of telltale signs such as unexpected charges, sudden outages in services, and dubious policies.

Using the Right Technology for Day Trading

Successful day traders are equipped with the right tools, and you should also be equipped with these basic equipment to ensure that your day trading investments will be worthwhile.

Reliable Computer

In day trading, the difference between profit and loss can be made in split seconds. Hence, it is crucial for day traders to be equipped with the latest technology in trading. You can be at a real disadvantage if you are using a sloppy computer to make your trades. But this doesn't mean that you should have the fastest computer available today, although that can help.

It is ideal to have a powerful computer that can run several applications and software at the same time without being cranky. You must have a computer that is equipped with high-quality CPU and a lot of RAM to make certain that you can run all the live data feeds, which you all need to follow along with the day trade charts as well as other data that will serve as your reference for you to decide in seconds. Laptops are okay, but tower computers are preferred.

It is also ideal to use powerful graphic cards, as you need one to efficiently power two monitors at the same time. Some day traders even need to run three monitors at the same time, so you don't have to switch screens when you are browsing for real-time updates. You may think that this is too much, but you will easily realize that you actually need one monitor for receiving news feeds, another for running the analytics software and another for the actual trading dashboard.

Reliable Internet Connection

Of course, you need to master how to use the trading platform you will use for your day trades. But without fast internet connection, your skills will be useless. It will be to your advantage if you are aware of your present bandwidth as well as the latency volume that your computer is experiencing. It is recommended that the latency volume is low. One solution for this is to work with a broker that is near your physical location, because the closer you are to the broker's server, the faster your trade will go through.

Moreover, you also have to consider secondary internet connection as a backup, so you can still trade if your main connection goes down. It should not be a dial-up connection, but it doesn't mean it should be as fast as your main line.

Source of Reliable Day Trading Information

It can be difficult to succeed in day trading if you are not well-informed. Remember, information is the prime commodity in the stock market. Although most of the information that you will need will depend on what strategies you are following and in what markets you are trading with, you should also take a closer look on the news to make certain that you are not missing out on any significant news or industry updates.

Even though there are many paid news subscriptions, you can still get by with free news feeds, especially with social media such as Facebook and Twitter. Try following industry influencers and other day traders.

Another source of information that you should always have is the Bloomberg Economic Calendar, which contains all relevant dates and upcoming deadlines for all big players in a particular market. As a day trader, you should be aware of these dates as trading without these guides can be a suicide.

Lastly, you might need to use a software or a website, which can work to narrow down possible trades that are worth analyzing further so that there is no need to spend all your time filtering the reliable news from garbage.

Don't Forget Your Health

As a day trader, you will mostly spend your time every day looking at several screens. Hence, it is crucial that you should also look after your health, so you can stay away from negative side effects that will come along with spending long hours in front of computer screens.

Recent studies show that standing while at work will increase your concentration levels and will also burn calories and avoid numerous types of adverse health effects. It is easy to find online some add-ons to your standard desk, which can change height easily, or you can also opt for a more complex option, which can elevate the height of the whole desk. Regardless of your preference, the sure thing is you can burn as much as 400 kcal in an average of eight hours of work per day.

Meanwhile, you should also take a break once in a while. Some day traders are also into meditation before they start the trade, or while taking a break.

Regardless of how much you make in day trading, it will all go to waste if you fail to look after yourself.

Conclusion

Day trading is a serious matter that you have to be prepared well before you get started. Getting into the trading platform without enough preparation and without the right tools and resources will only increase your chances of losing money.

So are you ready to start day trading? Not so fast. We still have to discuss the most common day trading strategies used by most traders today.

Chapter 4 - Entry Strategies for Day Trading

Expert day traders often look into two factors in choosing a stock - volatility and liquidity.

Volatility refers to the measurement of the projected daily price range or the range in which a day trader will operate. Higher volatility equals higher profit or loss. On the other hand, liquidity will allow you to enter and exit a stock at an ideal price, which can be tight spreads or the difference between the stock's ask and bid price, or lower slippage, or the difference between the trade's expected rate and the actual rate of the stock.

After knowing what types of stocks you are searching for, you also have to identify potential entry points. The entry tools that day traders commonly use are: candlesticks, Level II ECN, and News Subscription in Real Time.

Candlestick

Candles will allow you to look into the raw data for price movement. A candlestick refers to the chart, which shows the high, low, opening, and closing rates of a security for a certain period. This charting style originated in Japan where it was used in the 1700s to monitor the price of rice. Candlesticks are ideal tracking tools for financial assets with high liquidity such as forex, stock, and futures.

The larger portion of a candlestick is referred to as the real body, and it will tell you if the closing rate was lower or higher compared to the open rate. The black or red color will signify that the stock closed at a lower rate while green/white will signify that the stock closed at a higher rate.

The shadow of the candlestick will show the high and low price for the day, and how it compares to the opening and closing prices. The shape of the candlestick may vary according to the relationship between the high, low, closing and opening of the day's rates.

Candlesticks show the effect of the trader's sentiment on the prices of security and you can use this for technical analysis (which you will learn later on) to figure out if it is the right time to enter or exit the trades.

A long green/white candlestick signifies a prevalent buying pressure, which is often a sign of a bullish market. But you should look at them relative to the structure of the market as against individual trend.

For instance, a long white candlestick is regarded as more significant if its structure supports a primary price level. Meanwhile, long red/black candles signify that there is remarkable selling pressure, which is usually an indicator of a bearish market.

The usual bullish candle reversal pattern, regarded as a hammer, will form if the price movement is substantially lower after the opening, then will rally to close near the high. The hanging man is known as the equivalent bearish candlestick, which resembles a square lolly, and is usually utilized by day traders who are trying to find a bottom or top market.

Level II / ECN

Level II / ECN is a subscription-based service, which offers real-time access to the NASDAQ order catalog. This basically contains the price quotes from the market makers that are listed in OTC and NASDAQ securities. The Level II screen will show the bid prices as well as the sizes on the left and the ask rate and sizes on the right.

With Level II, you can have deep access to price information, which includes all the rates that market makers and Electronic Communication Network (ECN) are posting. Although Level I will only provide you with the best bid & ask rates, Level II will also show the supply & demand of the price levels that are beyond or outside the NBBO or National Best Bid Offer price. This will provide you a visual display of the price rate and related liquidity at every price level. Therefore, you can easily figure out entry and exit points, which will provide you the liquidity required to go for the exchange.

However, you should not always assume that the price movement on Level II is the real-time reflection of the exchanges that are recording. It is best to include the sales and time screen to monitor where the exchanges are being made. Level II is just a display of the available liquidity and price. This is still a critical information because the high-frequency trading programs regularly adjust Level II bid and ask rates violently to cause some commotion in spite of the lack of exchanges that are really happening on sales and time. This is a common strategy used for momentum trading.

Most ECNs enable traders to post reserve orders and concealed orders. Reverse orders are composed of a price & display size alongside the actual size. This order will only show the certain size of display on Level II as it conceals the actual total size of the order.

For instance, a day trader may like to sell 5,000 shares of ABC stock at $11.05, and the stock is selling at a bid of $11.025 with 250 shares and an asking rate of $11.05 with 50 shares displayed. If you post the 5,000 shares to sell on the asking rate at $11.05, this will repel the bidders at $11.025. They will assume that the seller is somehow desperate and may further drop the bid hoping for a better rate.

In posting a reserve order for selling 5,000 shares with 50 shares shown at $11.05, you can signify that there is limited supply on the asking rate. Buyers who are anxious may rush into the buying shares at $11.05, assuming that the price could increase by demand. The trade will be filled in with incremental value of 50 shares to the full 5000 shares before the upsticks and increase higher. Concealed orders may function the same way but they cannot be seen on Level II, which allows for more discretion to determine the rates. You can figure out if concealed or reserved orders are already filled in by checking the sales and time for trades at the signified prices.

News Analysis

News can influence the movement of stocks. The prices of stocks can fluctuate within minutes because of the changes in supply and demand. If many traders are buying a certain stock, the price in the market will go up. On the other hand, if many traders are selling a certain stock, the price in the market will go down. This behavior in supply and demand is related to the type of news reports that are announced at any certain period.

Bad news may usually cause investors to sell their stocks. Negative profit reports, damaged corporate governance, political and economic uncertainty, and sudden unfortunate events could lead to selling pressure and could result to lower prices of stocks.

Good news will usually cause investors to buy more stocks. Positive profit reports, efficient corporate affairs, corporate acquisitions or product launches, as well as great political and economic factors could lead to buying pressure and could result to higher prices of stocks.

However, it is usually hard, and not recommended to capitalize on news. The effect of new information on a stock will depend on how the news becomes unexpected. This is due to the fact that the market can always build future expectations into the prices. For instance, if the company emerges with better profits compared to its projections, the price of its stocks will likely go up.

Similarly, if the profit stays the same as expected by most of the investors, the price of the stock may likely stay the same as the profit will have been already considered in determining the price. Hence, it is sudden news, and not only any kind of news, which can help in driving prices.

Conclusion

It is crucial to identify specific stocks that are showing signs of positive movement. The best way to identify these stocks is through proven entry strategies such as using candlesticks, Level II ECN, and news analysis.

Chapter 5 - Technical Analysis in Day Trading

There are two types of methods used by professional day traders to analyze securities and help them in making investment decisions. These are technical analysis and fundamental analysis. The latter involves studying the basic nature of a company to make a projection of its value. On the other hand, Technical Analysis follows a completely distinct method. It does not take into account the value of the company and will only look into the movements of the price in the market.

In spite of all the remarkable tools used in Technical Analysis, it is really all about looking into the current supply and demand in the stock market, to determine what trend or direction will happen in the future. This style of analysis will allow you to understand the emotional factor in the market by looking into the market as a whole and not the individual movements. Understanding the advantages and restrictions of technical analysis can provide you with new set of tools as well as skills, which will allow you to become a better day trader.

In this Chapter, you will learn the fundamental concepts of technical analysis. It is quite a broad subject, which is worthy of another book, so we will just discuss the basics to provide you with the foundation you need so you will be able to make sense of more advanced topics as you go on with day trading.

Technical Analysis - The Basics

Technical Analysis refers to the strategy of studying securities by looking into the statistics representing the market activity such as the stock volume and past prices. In technical analysis, you don't have to make sense of the company's intrinsic value. You have to make sense of charts and use advanced tools so you can detect patterns that may continue in the near future.

There are different kinds of technical analysis. Some require the use of chart patterns, others depend on oscillators and technical indicators, while most use a mixture of these styles. Nonetheless, technical analysis is characterized by the exclusive use of historical price and volume information, which makes it distinctive from fundamental analysis.

Not similar to fundamental analysis, technical analysts do not really care if a particular stock is not valued enough. The only factor that you have to take into account is the historical data of the security and what information this data convey about where the security might be in the future.

There are three major assumptions that comprises the basis of Technical Analysis:

1. The prices of stocks move according to trends

2. History will repeat itself

3. The stock market will discount everything

Let's discuss each assumption in detail:

1. The Prices of Stocks Move According to Trends

The movement of stock prices according to trends is a fundamental concept in technical analysis. When the market is experiencing a trend, the possible movement of price in the future is more likely to be in similar movement of the trend than to be opposite of it. Many trading strategies founded on technical analysis are based on this assumption.

2. History Will Repeat Itself

Another crucial concept in technical analysis is that history has the tendency to repeat itself, mostly in terms of the movement of price. The replicability nature of the movement of prices is heavily related to psychological behavior of traders. Players in the market tend to provide a constant response to similar market stimuli in a certain period of time. In technical analysis, traders use chart patterns to study the movements in the market and make sense of current trends. Even though most of these charts have been used for centuries, these are still applicable because they show patterns in the movement of prices, which usually repeat over time.

This repetitive nature is applicable not only for stocks. It is also relevant to other securities such as forex, futures, commodities, and many more. In this book, we often cite stocks in our example, but you should bear in mind that this replicability is applicable to any kind of security. As a matter of fact, technical analysis is often associated with forex and commodities, where players are mostly day traders.

3. The Stock Market Will Discount Everything

A primary feedback about technical analysis is that it is only looking into the price movement, and it ignores the basic factors of the company. But an assumption of technical analysis points out that in any period, the price of a stock actually reflects everything that can have influence on the company, which includes the fundamental factors.

Day traders who are using technical analysis believe that the fundamental factors of the company, along with market psychology and economic factors, are all considered into the stock, which actually makes it unnecessary to look into these factors independently. Hence, the price movement is the only factor that should be looked into. Remember, according to the technical theory the price movement is the product of the demand and supply for a certain stock.

Technical Analysis versus Fundamental Analysis

After understanding the philosophy behind technical analysis, the next step is to understand how it really works. One way to look closely into the nature of technical analysis is to place it against fundamental analysis.

Fundamental analysis and technical analysis are the two primary strategies in studying the stock market. As we have already discussed above, technical analysis evaluates the movement of price of a certain security and uses this data to project the possible movements in the future.

On the other hand, fundamental analysis studies the economic indicators, which are known as fundamentals. We will discuss the specific of these two strategies - the main criticisms on technical analysis and how these two could be used to guide your decision in day trading.

The Differences between Technical Analysis and Fundamental Analysis

We can look into the differences between technical analysis and fundamental analysis if we take a closer look on their charts/financial statements, time horizon, and trading/investing.

Financial Statements and Charts

Basically, technical analysis is driven by charts, while fundamental analysis is driven by financial statements.

Through fundamental analysis, a trader can study the income statement, cash flow statement, and balance sheet to determine the value of the company. Financially, the trader can measure the intrinsic value of the company, which makes it actually easier to make a decision. If the stock price is being traded below the intrinsic value, then there is high possibility that the investment is good. Even though this can be overly simplified, (fundamental analysis is more than just poring over financial statements and balance sheets) for the sake of discussion in this book, this basic concept is true.

Through technical analysis, the trader does not consider the intrinsic value of the company, because of the assumption that these are all already integrated in the price of the stock. Day traders who are using technical analysis assume that all the information they need to make a decision are already manifested in the charts.

Time Horizon

More often than not, day traders who use fundamental analysis takes longer timeframe to analyze the market compared to day traders who are using technical analysis. While fundamental analysis usually looks into data in a span of years, technical analysis can be used for a time period of weeks, days, and even minutes.

The varying timeframes that these two strategies use is caused by the nature of the investment style that they follow. It may take years for the value of the company to reflect in the market. Hence, when a fundamental analyst project the intrinsic value, the gain will not be secured until the market price of the stock increases to match this value. This kind of investing is known as value investing, and it is based on the assumption that the short-term market is not true, and the price of a certain stock will rectify itself in due time. This "due time" could signify a timeframe of as long as several years, in certain instances.

Moreover, the numbers that a fundamentalist evaluates are only issued over longer time frames. The company's financial statements are filed every quarter and the changes in the profits per share are not reflected on an everyday basis such as price and volume data. You should also take note that the fundamentals are the actual nature of the business. Even though there is a new management team in the company, the changes will not be influential in the market overnight. It takes time to come up with new products, implement marketing campaigns, improve supply chains, and the like.

Hence, a part of the reason that fundamental analysis uses a long-term approach is because the data they use to analyze a stock is produced much slower compared to the volume and price data crucial in technical analysis.

<u>Investing / Trading</u>

Aside from the timeframe approach, fundamental analysis and technical analysis are also different in terms of the goals of a sale (or a purchase) of a certain stock. Generally, technical analysis is ideal for trading, while fundamental analysis is ideal for investment.

Stock investors purchase assets that they conclude could rise in value, while traders purchase asset that they conclude they could sell immediately at a higher price. The line between an investment and a trade could be blurry, but it can provide the distinction between the two stock concepts.

Criticisms against Technical Analysis

Some naysayers view technical analysis as a form of a forbidden tactic. In fact, some stock investors are questioning the validity of technical analysis as a true discipline. But as time goes by, technical analysis has seen support in the financial markets and has enjoyed mainstream credibility today. Even though most analysts in the financial markets are using fundamental analysis, many of them including large broker firms are now using technical analysis, too.

Much of the negative perception about technical analysis is rooted on the academic theories, particularly the EMH or the Efficient Market Hypothesis. EMH states that the price of the market is always the right price. Any previous trading data has been already considered in the current stock price and so, any attempt to look for undervalued stocks is unnecessary.

There are three versions of EMH:

1. Weak Form Efficiency

2. Semi-Strong Form Efficiency

3. Strong Form Efficiency

Weak Form Efficiency

In this version of EMH, all the data about the past stock prices are already factored in the prevailing price. Based on this version of EMH, you can project future movements through technical analysis, because the historical data have been all considered for, and so, analyzing the previous price movements of a particular stock will offer no insight for its future movements.

Semi-Strong Form Efficiency

In the second version of EMH, fundamental analysis is also considered as useless in searching for potential investment opportunities.

Strong Form Efficiency

This version of EMH claims that all data in the financial markets are all accounted for in the price of the stock and neither fundamental nor technical analysis could provide traders or investors with any advantage. Most financial analysts follow the weak form, thus, from its perspective, if technical analysis is effective, market efficiency can be called into question.

Conclusion

Even though fundamental analysis and technical analysis are regarded by most players in the financial markets as opposing sides - the water and oil in stock market - many players made substantial profits by using the two hand in hand.

For instance, there are fundamental investors who used technical analysis to determine the best time of entering into a security that is undervalued. Usually, this case happens if the security is highly over-sold. By identifying the best time to enter into security, the investor can increase his gains on the investment.

Comparatively, there are also technical traders who look at the company's fundamentals to validate the credibility of the technical indicator. For instance, if a selling indicator has been provided using technical strategies, a technical trader may look to validate the decision by searching at some core fundamental data. Usually, having both technical and fundamentals on your trading mix could provide you the best-case setting to get more profit out of the trade.

Chapter 6 - Day Trading Strategy: Scalping

Scalping is a day trading strategy that is characterized by making profits on small fluctuations in the market. This day trading strategy is often done right after the exchange has been completed and has become profitable. In scalping, you have to follow a stringent exit tactic, because a substantial loss will negate the many small profits, which you have already put a lot of effort to gain. To become a successful scalper, you must be equipped with the right tools like a live news feed, fast access to a reliable broker, and the decisiveness in placing many trades in a day.

Scalping Explained

Scalping is heavily based on the presumption that majority of stocks shall pass through the main stage of a movement. In other words, a stock will move in a specific direction for a short time, but where it goes from this location is still not certain. Some stocks will definitely continue moving forward, while others may cease to move.

As much as possible, you should take many small profits, and work on to hold them. This strategy actually go against the popular stock trading mindset of allowing your profits to run, which tries to optimize positive trading results by enhancing the profitable winning size while allowing others reverse.

Scalping can achieve positive results by growing the number of profits and not focusing too much on the size of the profit. It is fairly common for day traders who have been trading for a long time to achieve more profits by making only half or even lower of the trades.

Five Main Premises of Scalping

Below are the five primary premises of scalping as a strategy in day trading:

1. Smaller Movements Are More Frequent than Bigger Movements - Even during stable market conditions, there are still a lot of small fluctuations that a day trader can take advantage of to make small yet numerous profits.

2. Lower Exposure Equals Lower Risk - A shorter period of exposure to the market will lower the chance of experiencing substantial losses.

3. Smaller Movements Are Easier to Acquire - A greater imbalance of demand and supply is required to warrant larger price changes. Remember, it is easier for the market to make 10 cents move compared to a dollar movement.

4. Scalping Can Be Used As a Primary or Secondary Strategy in Day Trading

Scalping As a Primary Strategy in Day Trading

A professional scalper can make several trades every day between 10 and 1,000. If you decide to follow this strategy, you may need to use minute graphs and charts, because the time frame is limited and you have to look closely at the movement in real time. The essential tools for scalpers include the TotalView, Nasdaq Level II, or Times and Sales. It is also critical for a day trading scalper to execute fast orders, so a fast access to a broker is recommended.

Scalping As a Secondary Strategy in Day Trading

Scalping can also be used as a secondary strategy in day trading. The most popular way is to use this is during unstable market or if the market is experiencing lock down in a slim range. If there are no trends in a longer time period, going to a shorter time period could show visible and executable trends that could encourage day traders to scalp.

Another strategy to include scalping for a long-term strategy is through the concept known as "umbrella" strategy. This strategy will let you improve your cost basis as well as make more profit. In umbrella trading, the exchanges are performed in the following manner:

> 1. The trader will initiate a position for a long-term trade.

> 2. While the primary trade is developing, the trader will identify new setups in a shorter time frame to the direction of the primary trade, which enters and exits them through the scalping principles.

Basically for scalping, you can use any type of trading platform, which is based on certain setups. Hence, scalping is often regarded as a type of approach to manage risk. Any trade could be transformed into a scalp if you take a profit near the 1:1 reward/risk ratio, which means that the size of the profit is equal to the size of a stop that is mandated within the platform. For example, if you enter a position for scalping at $40 with an early stop at $39.50, then there is risk of 50 cents, so the reward/risk ratio could be achieve at $40.50.

You can perform scalping on either short or long sides. You can perform them on range-bound or breakouts. Most conventional charts like triangles, handles, or cups could be suitable for scalping. This is also true for technical indicators if you wish to refer them in making your decisions.

3 Major Types of Day Trading Scalping

There are three major types of scalping strategy that you can use for day trading: market making, large purchasing, and position closing.

1. <u>Market Making</u> - This type of scalping strategy will allow you to leverage on the spread by posting the bid and offer simultaneously for a certain stock. Market making will only be effective for immobile stocks, which are exchanged in large volumes without any changes in the actual price. This type of scalping is largely difficult to perform, because you have to deal with the competition against market makers for the stocks on the offers and bids. In addition, the potential profit can be minimal that any movement in the stock opposing to your position could lead to losses that are over your original revenue target.

2. <u>Large Purchasing</u> - This type is done by buying a substantial amount of shares, which are traded for a gain on slim price fluctuations. In this scalping style, you have to enter into position for hundreds to thousands shares and wait for small movement, which is often measured in cents. This approach will require stocks that are highly liquid to allow for easy entering and exiting thousands of shares.

3. <u>Position Closing</u> - This type of scalping strategy is considered closest to the conventional forms of stock trading. In this style, you have to enter an

amount of shares on any signal or setup from your system, and close the position as the main exit signal is generated near the 1:1 reward/risk ratio, computed as discussed earlier.

Conclusion

Scalping could be a very lucrative strategy for day traders who want to use this as a primary trading strategy, or even traders who want a supplementary strategy in trading. Following the stringent exit strategy is a critical point to make the small profits compounded into substantial profits. The short amount of exposure to the market as well as the frequency of small movements are core characteristics that are the main reason why this strategy is common even among those who are not into day trading.

Chapter 7 - Day Trading Strategy: Fading

Fading is a day trading strategy, which is characterized by trading contrary to the current trend in the market. This strategy is usually a very risky strategy, which requires you to have high level of risk tolerance. In fading strategy, you have to sell if the price is rising and buy if the price is falling.

Fading Strategy Explained

An example of fading is purchasing on a dip in price then selling if the price increases. There is high volatility in this strategy, but there is high potential for remarkable gains. This requires less complicated analysis, but the risk, which the trend will continue is always there.

For instance, if there is a better bid available on another exchange for stock and the market makers are not willing or not able to go for it for the trade, they may offer to exchange with other market makers on a better price. Market makers who are selling the stocks at a higher price should go for the offer and exchange at the rate provided or make adjustments in the price at bid.

The Trade or Fade Rule

More often than not, fading strategy is ideal for day traders who have just learned about a significant news on particular markets, especially in forex. The line of thinking is that after the first wave or price increase the retracement or pull back could happen, and they could initiate fading.

You should remember that in trading against the current trend, regardless if you are on a longer or shot term chart, you have to deal with added risk. This is a major problem in trading against the trend, because the longer term trend could be retraced at any given time.

If you use the fading strategy in a falling price, you have to wait for the prices to stall its fluctuation to the downtrend and fade the move by buying stocks or currency pairs. This is why the fading strategy is suitable for day traders who are more open to take risks and can deal with common emotions related in going against the market. Traders are fading stocks because most of the gains are seen in the initial movement of the price, if everyone else is not willing to take a stand. If the fading strategy is handled properly, the day trader can be profitable, especially in calling a market bottom.

Purchasing the Dip

Purchasing the dip refers to the condition that the stock has a breakdown based on a support level and rather than selling the break, the day trader will stand on a longer position. The thought process here is that the market usually has no sufficient trading pressure to maintain the downtrend and that the prices will eventually rise.

Trading the Breakout

There are many forms of market tops, but these are usually preceded by a false break before going uptrend. Day traders usually fade during the breakouts by watching over the clear swing highs where a stock could clear the level with minimal price action and light volume. This signifies that there is minimal trading pressure, and the stock will imminently fall down.

Conclusion

Using the fading strategy for day trading is a risky style, so it is ideal to follow a certain method of opposing the trend. You can learn more about what to do through technical analysis. If the stock starts to sell off, you should have a good reason to stand your ground. You can take advantage of tools such as the oscillator (MACD), which can help you make sense of initial indicators that the downturn is losing its stream. As a day trader, you can use this tool to take a long-term position to anticipate the changes in the trend.

Chapter 8 - Day Trading Strategy: Daily Pivots

Pivot points are analyzed by day traders to find a standard support and resistance factor on the chart showing the price of a particular stock.

Once a price action achieves a pivot level, it can be extended (breakout) or supported (resistance). Day traders still consider the situation normally even if the price action is approaching a pivot point on the chart. When the stock price begins hesitating in reaching this level and abruptly bounces in the opposing direction, day traders often trade according to the bounce's direction.

If the price action is breaking through pivots, however, then there is a higher chance that the action shall continue to the breakout's direction. If the price clears the level, this will be known as a breakout pivot point.

How Day Traders Use Pivot Points

After understanding the basic framework of pivot points, the next step is to take a closer look into two primary strategies in day trading - pivot level breakouts and pivot point bounces.

Pivot Point Bounces

This pivot point trading approach is characterized by the price action bouncing from the pivot levels. In this approach, day traders usually open trades if the price reaches a pivot point then bounces.

By following this approach, you should buy a stock if it is testing a pivot line from the top side then bounces upward.

Similarly, it is ideal to short the security if the price is testing the pivot line from the bottom and bounces downward.

For this trade, the stop-loss order must be situated below if you are long and above the pivot level if you are short.

 The chart above shows the five-minute movement of the stock of Ford Motors on 14 July 2016. The chart reveals two pivot points bouncing exchange based on the approach described above.

Based on our analysis of the pivot points, the first trade begins five periods after opening the market. The price hits above R2 in the opening bell, then a decrease was experienced then bounced from the level of R2, which created a long indicator on the chart, and the trader purchased the Ford stocks on a stop loss order under level R2.

As you can see, the price experiences a bullish trend and so it is ideal to maintain the trade until the stock reaches the level R3, which you can close once this occurs. But take note that the price bounces downwards from the level R3, which is another bouncing pivot point, so we can short the stock following our strategy. As shown in the chart, the trader placed a stop-loss order on level R3.

Ford suddenly experienced a bearish trend after a brief consolidation and another cycle and a bounce originating from level R3. The trader can hold the short trade until Ford will touch the level R2 and makes an exit indicator.

Pivot Point Breakouts

It is important to open a position if the price breaks through a point pivot level so you can enter a point pivot breakout trade.

A short trade is ideal if the stock price trend is bearish, and a long trade is ideal if the breakout is bullish. A stop loss is also ideal if you are trading pivot points breakouts. A recommended place for the stop is a top-bottom that is situated prior to the breakout. Through this, the trade can always be secured against sudden price movements.

Below is a five-minute chart for Bank of America from 25 to 26 July 2016. The chart shows bullish trend taken according to the pivot point strategy for breakout.

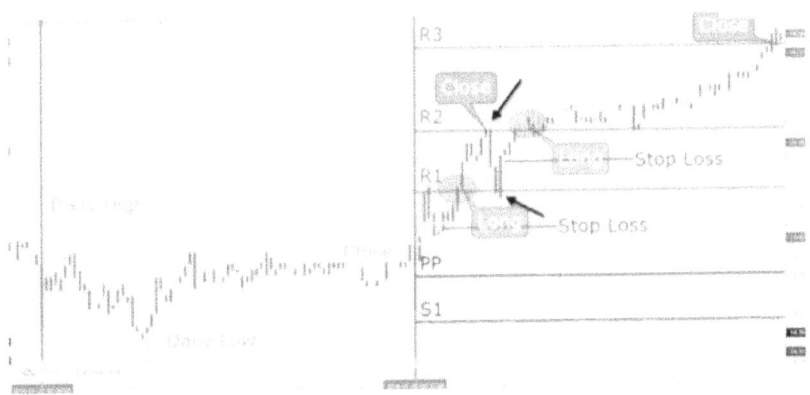

The first red circle on the chart highlights the stock's breakout in the level R1. In this case, the day traders would have to go long and place a stop loss order under the past bottom under the pivot point on R1. Take note that the stock price rises suddenly after the pivot.

It is ideal to hold the trade until the price action will reach the next pivot point on the chart. If this occurs, the price will create two swing bounces from R2 level and R1 level. After the bounce from R1, the price will increase and will break through R2. This results to another long signal on the chart. Hence, it is best to purchase the stock again.

Take note of the long candlewick under level R2 that is ideal for the stop-loss order. The stock price starts to hesitate on top of the level R2. In the last minutes of the trading session, the BAC rises again and will reach level R3 before the session's end. This is the exit indicator, which prompts the traders to close the trade.

The Advantages of Using Pivot Points for Day Trading

1. Pivot Points is Unique for Day Trading

The formula for pivot points takes the information from the past trading day and applies it to the present trading day. With this strategy, the levels that you are searching at are relevant only to the present trading day. Hence, pivot points become the ultimate indicator for day traders.

2. High Level of Accuracy

Pivot point as an indicator, is regarded as one of the most accurate tools in day trading, mainly because these are used mostly by day traders. Hence, you can trade with high accuracy for the general market flow.

3. Rich Data Set

On charts, the pivot points offer a rich data set. As already discussed in this Chapter, the signal can provide seven separate trading levels. This is certainly sufficient to take a day trader using the trading session.

4. Ease of Use

The Pivot Point indicator is easy to use, even for beginners. Many of the trading platforms provide this form of indicator. Hence, it is not necessary to compute the separate levels, because the trading platform will already do this for you. You just need to trade the breakouts and the bounces of the signals.

5. Shorter Trading Period

Because the data for pivot points is from one trading day, the indicator is only relevant to short time frames. Hence, the 30-minute and daily chart will not work, because it will only show single or double candles. The ideal time frames for the pivot indicators are 15-minute, five-minute, two-minute, and one-minute.

Conclusion

As a day trader, you should master how to use pivot points as your reference in identifying which specific stocks to trade. Using pivot points will increase your trading accuracy as well as profitability.

Chapter 9 - Day Trading Strategy: Momentum

In stock indicators, momentum measures the rate of the fall or rise in stock prices. From this perception of trending, momentum is a necessary indicator of weakness or strength in the price of the stock. Based on historical data, momentum is proven more useful during the upward trend in the market compared to a downward market.

The main reason for this is that the markets follow an upward trend than they follow a downward trend. To put this simply, bull markets have the tendency to last longer in comparison with bearish markets.

Technical analysts utilize a ten-day time period to measure momentum. You will often see the zero line in most charts. When the most recent closing price of the stock is more than the closing price for the previous 10 days, the positive number from the formula is plotted on top of the zero line. Meanwhile, if the latest closing rate is lower compared to the closing rate 10 days ago, the negative measurement will be placed under the zero line.

In taking the measurement of the price differences over a certain period of time, you can begin to take note of the prices at which the stock is falling or rising. Momentum can help you identify the trend lines.

Specific trend lines can develop as the price of stock increases, while an upward momentum plot line on top of the zero signifies that a rising trend is strongly developing. If the plot line is beginning to level off, this signifies to technical analysts that the latest stock price is about the same as it was 10 days ago. Hence, the trend's velocity is slacking. The reverse situation can also be true.

As a beginner in day trading, you should understand that if the momentum indicator slides downwards under the zero line and then will reverse in a rising direction. This doesn't mean that the falling trend will be completed. This can only mean that the falling trend is also slacking down. It is also true if the plotted momentum is on top of the zero line.

Below are several techniques, which you can use to become more successful in momentum trading:

Entry Techniques

To determine the inertia in the market, day traders can use EMA or Exponential Moving Average to find the downtrends and uptrends. If EMA rises, the inertia will favor the bullish market, and if the EMA falls, the inertia will favor a bearish market.

In measuring market momentum, the trader can use the MACD (moving-average-convergence-divergence) histogram. MACD is an oscillator that displays a slope showing the changes of power between the bears and bulls.

If the slope of the MACD shows uptrend, the bulls are becoming more dominant. If the slope of the MACD shows downtrend, the bears are becoming more dominant.

The impulse system will issue an entry indicator if both the momentum and inertia signals are moving in the same direction, and the exit signal is issued if these two signals become divergent.

If the indicators from both the MACD and EMA are pointing in one direction, the momentum and inertia are working together towards the obvious downtrends and uptrends. If both the MACD and EMA, the market is bearish and so a downtrend is imminent.

Below is a sample chart showing an MACD with 9-period EMA.

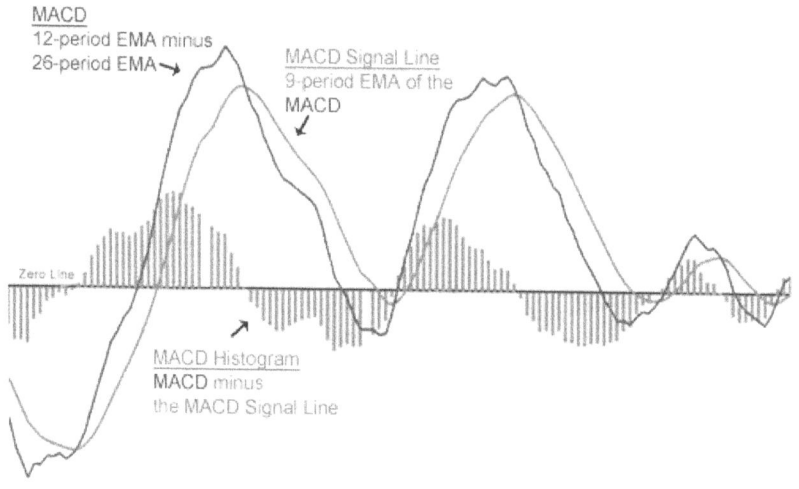

Exit Techniques

The primary reason why momentum trading is effective in both strong and sloppy markets is that you are searching a short-term momentum and not a longer one. Financial markets usually trend within any week, and the ideal stocks to trade are those that are regularly showing strong intra-day trends. In this case, you should take note to step off the momentum before it peaks.

As we have already discussed, when you have determined and entered into a strong momentum trading opportunity (if daily MACD and EMA are both following an uptrend), you must exit the position at the very moment that the indicator is turning down. The MACD for the day is often the first to turn, as the rising momentum starts to weaken. However, this may not be a genuine selling indicator of the removal of the buying indicator. In using the impulse system, this indicator is not enough for selling.

Take note that if the weekly trend is falling, and the daily MACD and EMA are falling while you are in short position, you must cover the shorts as soon as possible for the indicators to stop a selling indicator, if the downtrend momentum has stopped the fasted part of the descent. The best time to sell is before the trend reaches the absolute bottom. In contrast with a selected entry point, the exit points will require fast actions at the particular moment that your determined trend will appear the nearing end.

Conclusion

Mental strength and concentration are crucial if you want to use momentum in day trading. This will allow you to stay steadfast if things are moving as expected and wait once the targets are ready to be achieved. Day trading using momentum also requires strong discipline, a unique trait that makes short-term momentum among the most difficult strategies of making profit.

Chapter 10 - Creating Your Own Day Trading Plan

A day trading plan is an essential tool to become more successful in any financial market. Without a plan, you are just gambling. In this Chapter, we will learn how to make a trading plan.

A day trading plan will also provide you an objective viewpoint whether your trading strategy is working or not. It can be very difficult to determine if you are profitable or not if you don't have a plan. By following a trading plan, you will always have a reason why you are making a trade.

What Is a Day Trading Plan?

There are three basic section in a day trading plan:

1. Entry Rules

2. Exit Rules

3. Fund Management

These three sections work together to create a system, which is suitable for your personality and that you will actually follow. Rules that you are always breaking are futile. Hence, before writing rules for entry, exit, and fund management, you should also take a personal inventory. Your trading plan rules are built upon these crucial decisions.

You can also use the trading plan to determine which financial market you want to trade. Should you go for futures, stocks, forex, or options? You can make a lot of profit from these markets, but they are not the same. Every market has various starting fund requisites and when they are open for trade may vary. You should always choose one and stick with it. Never try to learn all markets at the same time.

Determine Your Time Constraints

Day trading can be difficult if you have a day job, although it is still possible to make trades. It is ideal to concentrate on one strategy for day trading where you could look for trades at night and place your orders for the next day. You should decide when you will search for possible trades or when you will place your orders. Be sure to build your plan around this strategy.

Determine Your Capital Constraints

As mentioned earlier, the markets have various beginning fund requirements or recommendations. The stocks tend to be the most capital intensive for trading. Stock market is ideal if you have less than $30,000 for trading. Never trade the market if you don't have enough fund. Underfunding will become clearer if we discuss managing money in the next section. If you don't have enough money for the market you want to trade, you should wait until you have more fund. Take note that you can still establish your trading plan and try to practice a demo account.

Entry Rules

Entry rules will comprehensively point out what has to happen so you can penetrate a position. This series of events may include certain movements for price, statistics, chat patterns, indicators, or any other factor that you feel will place you on the proper side of the market. You should include in the entry rules section if you want to trade short and/or long side of the market.

Try answering the questions below and then integrate them into your day trading plan:

- o What general market settings should be present to enter a trade?

- o Are there certain conditions that you will not take a signal?

- o What specific chart times will you keep track?

- o Are trades completed as soon as the signal happens?

- o Are there delays in taking the position at the end of the trading day?

Be sure to keep the entry rules simple and easy to remember, so you can easily make a decision. You might have the tendency to make mistakes or freeze in crucial moments if your rules are complicated.

Exit Rules

Exit Rules comprehensively outline what should happen for you to exit a trade. These rules should include the chart patterns, price movements, signals, or reversal of the first signal that caused the entry. This section in your day trading plan should outline how and where a stop loss is placed. A stop loss is an order, which can get you out of a losing trade if a specific price has been achieved. This section will also decide if you will use a profit targets, which is an order that will get you out of the trade if a certain price has been achieved.

Money Management

The day trading plan is established from the ground up according to your personal financial risk. A possibly winning strategy, which involves too much risk based on money management rules means that the strategy is not effective. Day trading strategies should be customized according to your resources and needs. Hence, you should begin by stating how much fund you have available for trading.

It is recommended that no more than 1 per cent of your capital must be risked on one trade. When a strategy is validated as effective, you can increase this limit to 2% maximum. However, most day traders keep the risk under 1% for each trade. If you have $50,000 in trading fund, $500 is the highest limit for every trade.

If the trade is risky (higher than $500) between the entry & exit, you should not take the trade. Take note of the risk on the capital value to figure out the number of shares in the stock market you could take if you know the price for the trade's entry as well as stop-loss.

As your trading fund increases, the value risked on every trade will also increase. Basically, this is because 1 per cent of $50,000 is higher than the 1 per cent of $ 25000. Hence, your percentage risk will always stay the same for every trade. However, as your fund grows, the value that you are risking will become higher, possibly resulting to higher dollar gains. If your fund falls because of losses, the value risked on every trade will also decrease. Even though the percent of the account at risk will remain.

Putting It All Together

After completing your trading plan, the next step is to start implementing it. This is where you can test your plan if the rules you have laid out are profitable or not. Let us examine a sample trade that you may encounter as you start your testing for your trading plan.

Let's say that you have selected to trade in stocks and you are willing to lose a max of $500 for every trade based on your $50,000 fund. You have seen a setup on a trade, which is aligned on your rules for entry on AABB that trades at $40. The chart patterns, technical analysis, and the rules for exit shall signify that you should place a stop loss at $39.50, which will expose the trade at a possible $0.50 downtrend movement of the stock.

In this case, you might also need to take a look at what your possible profit is, to ensure the possible profit can even guarantee the trade. Let's say that you have figured out that an ideal target for profit is $41. If you reach the target, you can make a dollar for every share, and you have only risked 50 cents to achieve it. The possible reward is double, so you can pursue the trade.

Based on this you could then figure out the number of shares you want to buy, so the risk is actually below $500. By purchasing at least 500 shares, you can hit the stop, so you may lose a $500 exclusive of fees and commissions. Hence, if you are factoring the fees and commission, you should also run down the stocks you want to purchase. In such case, you can buy at least 400 units at $40 ($16,000 in cost) and put a stop-loss at $39.50, which will expose you to $200 in risk plus commissions. The profit target, if you are selecting one, will be ordered in this moment.

You can manage the trade by keeping track of the rules for exiting the trade. When the trade triggers the exit rules, be sure to exit the way you have already described in your plan. If there are other available trades, these might or might not be ordered according to the rules you have written in your day trading plan.

Conclusion

A day trading plan is a way for you to be objective in trading the stock market in a manner, which is suitable for your financial situation and individual personality. This plan will outline everything, which should occur in order to enter an exchange, and everything required for the trade exit. These factors are administered by your rules for money management that mitigates the risk on every trade lower than 1% for your trading fund.

Chapter 11 - Success Tips in Day Trading

Most beginners in day trading who want to learn how to become profitable in the stock market need only to spend several minutes online before they can read familiar maxims such as "minimize your losses" and "trade your plan; plan your trade." For those who are only starting in the trade, these gems of wisdom might seem more like a distraction than an advice for action. Beginners usually just want to know how to draw their charts, so they can move on and make profits.

But to become profitable in stock day trading, you should understand the essence of and follow a set of rules, which have guided all kinds of traders with a variety of trading account sizes. Every rule is crucial, but if they are tied together, the impact can be strong. Day trading with these success rules can significantly increase the odds of becoming profitable in the stock market.

Success Tip No. 1 - Follow Your Day Trading Plan

We have already discussed in the previous chapter the importance of setting a day trading plan. The next step is to follow it. With the latest software for day trading, you can test a trading idea before you can risk real money. In back testing, you can apply trading ideas to historical data, and allow traders to figure out if a trading plan is effective, and also shows the viability of the plan.

When you have developed the plan and the backtesting displays remarkable results, you can use the plan for the actual trade. The essence here is to stick to the plan. Making trades outside the trading plan, despite them being profitable, is regarded as poor trading, and will damage the expectancy that you have in the plan.

Success Tip No. 2 - Leverage on the Power of Technology to Increase Your Edge

Day trading is a very competitive industry, and your competitors (other day traders) are using advanced technology to take advantage of the trade. Charting software will allow you to trade using different methods to view and analyze the market. You can backtest the trade based on historical data before risking any fund, so you can save a trading account. This is not to mention disappointment and stress. You can also use your smartphone to get market updates anytime and anywhere. Even technological advancements that we ignore today such as high-speed connections, could significantly increase your performance for trading.

Success Tip No. 3 - Treat Day Trading Like a Business

Whether you engage in day trading on a part-time or full-time, you should always treat it as a business. Never consider this as a hobby, where you don't have real commitment. In fact, trading as a hobby can be expensive. As a day job, day trading can be disappointing, because you can't expect for a regular paycheck. Treat day trading as a business, as you are also incurring expenses, risk, losses, uncertainty, taxes, and undetermined profit. As a day trader, you are basically a small business owner, and you should do your background research and create strategies to maximize the potential of your business.

Success Tip No. 4 - Study the Stock Market Continuously

You can consider studying the stock market as part of your continuing education as a professional day trader. Day traders should be focused on learning more every day. Because most concepts are carrying background knowledge, it is crucial to remember that studying the markets, and all its intricacies, is a continuing, and lifetime process.

Solid research will allow you to learn the fact, similar to what the various economic reports will mean. Observation and concentration will allow day traders to achieve instinct and learn the nuances. This will help you understand how the economic news influence the stock market.

Global politics, economies, important events - even the traffic - all have an effect on the markets. The market setting is dynamic. The more day traders understand the previous and present stock markets.

Success Tip No. 5 - Create a Day Trading Approach Based on Facts

Taking the time to create an effective trading methodology is worth your effort. Many beginner day traders are enticed to believe in the "stock trading" scams that are very prevalent today online. However, the facts, not hope or emotions, must be the basis behind creating your trading plan.

Day traders who are not in a rush in learning usually have an easier time browsing through all the data available online. Just think about this: if you were to begin a new career, you might need to study at a university or a college to earn a degree relevant to the career before you even become qualified to apply for a position in the field. You should expect that learning how to trade will demand at least the same value of time and will factually drive research and learning.

Success Tip No. 6 - Know When You Should Stop the Trade

There are two primary reasons why you should stop the trade: if the trader is not effective or if the trading plan is not effective. A trading plan that is not effective will show much significant loss compared to the expected historical testing. Markets could change, volatility within a specific trading instrument could have decreased, or the trading plan is merely not performing as expected. You can benefit by considering the trade as a business and don't be too emotional about it. It is best to re-evaluate the trading plan and make some changes, or to begin over with a new plan for day trading. A trading plan that is not successful is a problem, which you should solve, and doesn't mean that you should end your day trading.

Success Tip No. 7 - Guard Your Trading Fund

Saving money to finance a trading account may take a long time and effort. This can even be nearly impossible the next time you trade. It is crucial to note that safeguarding your fund is not equal with not having any losing trades. All day traders have losing trades, and this is normal in any business. Safeguarding your fund will entail not taking any unnecessary risks and you should do everything you can to guard your day trading business.

Success Tip No. 8 - Trade Only What You Are Willing to Lose

As we have already discussed, financing a day trading account could take a lot of time and effort. Before a day trade starts using real money, it is crucial that all of the cash in the account be really expendable. If not, the trader must keep saving until it becomes expendable.

Hence, the fund in a day trading account should not be allocated for the college tuition of your kids or for mortgage settlement. You should never allow yourself to think that you are just borrowing money from these other crucial necessities. You should be willing to lose all these money allocated to a day trading account.

Losing money for a day trading can be traumatic, and it can be worsened by the fact that the capital must have never been risked in the trade.

Success Tip No. 9 - Always Place a Stop-Loss Order

A stop loss refers to a predetermined value of risk that you are willing to accept for every trade. The stop loss could either be a dollar value or percentage, but in any case it can limit the exposure of the trader during a trade. Using a stop loss could take some emotion out of the trade, because we already know that we can only lose a certain amount on any specific trade.

It is considered bad practice to ignore a stop loss, even if the trade becomes profitable. Exiting with a stop loss in place, and so having a losing trade, is still considered as a good practice, if it has been done within the day trading plan. Although the ideal setting is to exit all the trades with a profit, it is not always possible. You can use a protective stop loss to make certain that your losses and risks will be limited.

Success Tip No. 10 - Focus on the Big Picture

It is crucial to be focused on the big picture if you are in day trading. A losing trade must not be a surprise, because it is part of the trade. Similarly, a winning trade is just another step along the path to become profitable. This refers to a cumulative profit, which make it unique. When you accept losses and wins as part of the day trading business, your emotions will have less of an impact on trading performance. This doesn't mean that you can't be thrilled about a certain profitable trade, but you should bear in mind that a losing trade might not be far off.

Conclusion

By taking a closer look on the significance of each of these trading rules, and how they are working together, you can establish profitable trading business. Take note that day trading requires hard work, and those who have the patience and the discipline in following these rules could increase their chances for success in a very competitive industry.

Conclusion

Thanks again for taking the time to download this book!

By now, you should have a good understanding of how you can use stock trading business to start your day trading as a business.

The next step is to work on your day trading plan, stick to it, and start receiving your rewards as a professional day trader.

www.ingramcontent.com/pod-product-compliance
Lightning Source LLC
Chambersburg PA
CBHW061205180526
45170CB00002B/972